Me and My Pet

Rabbits

How to train your own

UNIVERSITY PRESS

OXFORD
UNIVERSITY PRESS

Great Clarendon Street, Oxford OX2 6DP

Oxford University Press is a department of the University of Oxford.
It furthers the University's objective of excellence in research, scholarship,
and education by publishing worldwide in

Oxford   New York

Auckland   Cape Town   Dar es Salaam   Hong Kong   Karachi
Kuala Lumpur   Madrid   Melbourne   Mexico City   Nairobi
New Delhi   Shanghai   Taipei   Toronto

With offices in

Argentina   Austria   Brazil   Chile   Czech Republic   France   Greece
Guatemala   Hungary   Italy   Japan   Poland   Portugal   Singapore
South Korea   Switzerland   Thailand   Turkey   Ukraine   Vietnam

Oxford is a registered trade mark of Oxford University Press
in the UK and in certain other countries

British Library Cataloguing in Publication Data

Data available

ISBN-13: 978-0-19-911583-9

1 3 5 7 9 10 8 6 4 2

Printed in Singapore by Imago

MEET LULU

Name: Lulu McGregor
Age: 9 months
Breed: Dutch
Lives: Edinburgh, Scotland
Owners: Dan and Polly McGregor,
                 ages 8 and 6

I am writing this for Dan and Polly and their friends,
so that they understand me and we can all live happily together.

Lulu

Look at me!

My name is Lulu and I'm very friendly. I love having a human to look after and follow around. I can live in the house or in a hutch in the garden, but I do need friends. If I can't share my home with another rabbit, I need my human to come and play with me every day.

My **eyes** are on the sides of my head, so I can look behind me to see if anything is getting too close. The trouble is, this means I can't see what's in front of my nose unless I dip my head!

My **nose** is clean and twitchy.

My **teeth** will grow all through my life. I need some hard food, such as Brussel sprouts or a root vegetable, to gnaw on and stop my teeth from growing too long.

My **ears** can turn to help me listen. I
prick them up, so they stand up straight.

I need to get some **exercise** every day otherwise I'll
get fat and lazy. I love to run around on the grass.
Sometimes, I like to **dig** and will make holes
in the garden unless you stop me!

My **fur** is smooth and glossy. If I get
bald patches, take me to the vet.

I have soft fur close to my skin
to keep me warm and longer
guard hairs that stop my skin
getting scratched.

I like to keep my **toes** and **nails** clean. If they
are red or look sore, please take me to the vet.

My back **feet** are longer than my front ones so I move in
a leap-frogging way. If I'm scared I can move very quickly,
but I get very tired and can't do it for long.

Different breeds

I'm a Dutch rabbit but we come in many different shapes and sizes.

Lop rabbits, like my friend Penelope, have really long ears! These rabbits' ears are so heavy that they can't prick them up like me. This means they don't hear as well as I do. French lop rabbits can be very grumpy and bad-tempered.

Netherland Dwarf
rabbits make great pets.
They have small, round
heads and short ears.
Netherland Dwarf rabbits
only weigh about as much
as a bag of sugar.

Angoras usually have long white hair and pink eyes as they
are albino. Their long fur can be spun into wool. Angoras need
to have their fur combed regularly to stop it getting tangled.

Satin rabbits have very shiny coats. They come in lots of different colours.

The **Flemish Giant** is enormous. It can weigh up to 10 kg,
that's the same as 10 fully grown Netherland Dwarf rabbits.

My family

I come from a big family. I'm related to all the other rabbit breeds in the world. My other relatives are hares and pikas.

Hares are usually shy creatures, but go a bit mad in the spring and can be seen chasing each other across meadows. Sometimes male hares will box with one another. They are usually fighting for a female.

Hares can run much faster than rabbits.
They can reach speeds of up to 70 km an hour.

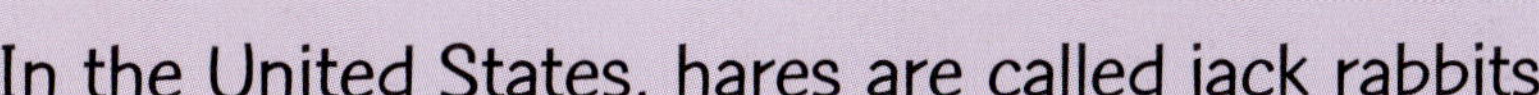

In the United States, hares are called jack rabbits

Pikas look more like hamsters than rabbits, but they are related to me. They are sometimes called '**whistling hares**' because of the high-pitched alarm call they make when they are frightened.

Pikas are friendly animals and live in family groups. They help each other collect food and **snuggle** up together to keep warm.

Pikas like to **sunbathe** in warm weather. Their fur is the same colour as the rocks on which they rest. This makes them difficult to spot and keeps them safe from predators.

I am born

We rabbits love big families and will have lots of babies, if you let us. Female rabbits, like my mum, are called does. They can start having babies when they are just four months old and can have more than 50 babies in a year. Baby rabbits are sometimes called kittens.

The baby rabbits are born about 30 days after the doe and the buck (male rabbit) have mated.

While she is pregnant, the doe will make a cosy nest for her babies. She pulls bits of fur from her coat to line the nest and keep her babies warm.

Baby rabbits are usually born at night. Does usually give birth to five young, but there can be as many as ten.

Pregnant does need a lot of food to make their babies strong and healthy. Just before her babies are born, she will be eating about twice as much food as before.

The mother **licks** her babies clean and then feeds them on her rich milk.

Baby rabbits are **helpless** when they are born. Their ears and **eyes are closed** and they only have a thin covering of **fur**. They need their mother to keep them warm and safe.

When they are about a **week old**, baby rabbits start to grow thicker fur.

After about **ten days**, baby rabbits open their eyes. Their ears open about two days later.

By about **16 days**, the young rabbits are becoming curious and will start exploring outside the nest. They will also start to nibble solid food, but they need their mum's milk until they are about eight weeks old.

After the babies are born, try not to disturb the mother and her young. Do not try to pick up the babies or play with them. If the mother gets disturbed or upset, she may kill her babies.

Choosing our owners

By the time we are about eight to twelve weeks old, we are ready to find a new home. We are easy to pick up and cuddle, and if you are gentle, we will love it. This helps us to get used to humans and stops us from being shy.

I like **company** and love having one of my sisters around. My brothers are fine too, if they have been neutered.

Young **male** rabbits should be housed on their own from this age, otherwise they get grumpy and start fighting.

I need a good, roomy **hutch** to live in. It should have two big rooms connected together. One of the rooms should be light and airy, so that I can see out and watch what's happening. The other room should have a solid door to give me shelter from the wind or rain. I'll sleep in the sheltered side too.

Place my hutch off the ground so that I don't get damp. This also protects me from rats and nosey dogs.

When I live with you, please keep an eye on the weather. If it's very hot, I will need shade. And if it's very cold, wet, or windy I will need shelter.

I do like to keep clean, so please clean out my hutch two or three times a week.

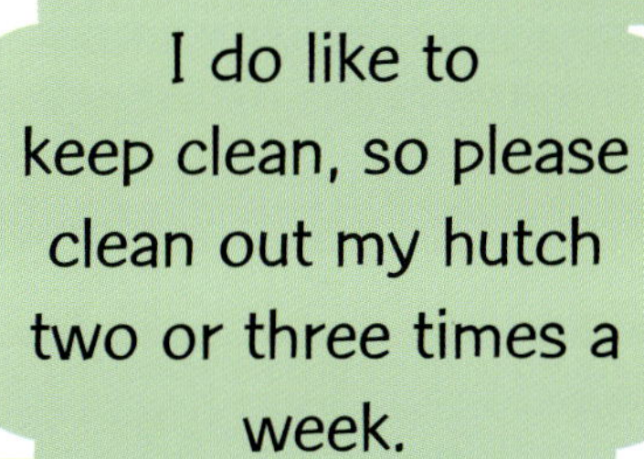

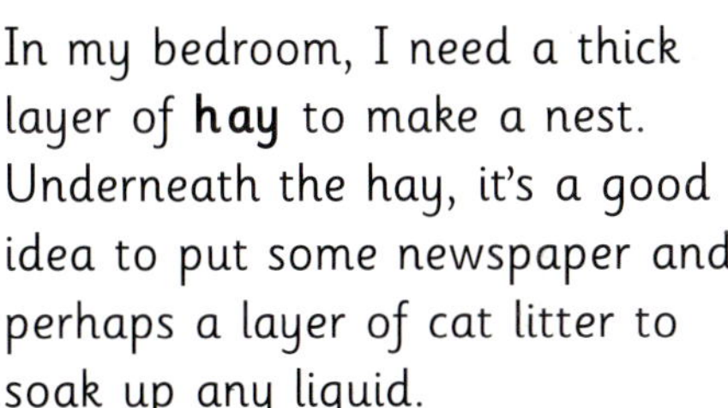

In my bedroom, I need a thick layer of **hay** to make a nest. Underneath the hay, it's a good idea to put some newspaper and perhaps a layer of cat litter to soak up any liquid.

I always need to **drink water**. Please make sure I have plenty of fresh water all the time. A bottle with a drip-feed is best, as I spill water in bowls and make a mess.

I need some **exercise** every day. It's best if you make a run for me, so that I can't escape and hide in the garden. Please keep an eye on me though. Other animals may come into the garden and frighten me.

Learning through play

I do like to play with my owners, Dan and Polly, and enjoy being picked up and cuddled gently. Very young children are too tiring for me, so I prefer to live with families with school-age children.

I can get overtired if Dan and Polly pet me too much and this may make me grumpy. If I start looking fed up, or am struggling to get away, please put me down on the grass.

You can pick me up by grasping the loose fur at the **scruff of my neck**. Scoop your other hand under my rump to help support my weight. I like it best if I am cradled close to your chest. Once I'm used to being picked up and carried, you can pick me up by putting one hand under my chest and the other under my rump. I prefer this as I feel much safer. **Never** pick me up by my **ears**.

When you are putting me back in my hutch, I like to go in back **feet first**. This means that if I forget my manners or get a bit frightened, I won't kick or scratch you. I prefer to keep my **feet on the floor** and really like it when you get down to my level to talk to me. That way, if I'm scared, I can run away.

If I'm in my cage for a long time, I can get a bit bored. I like to **play** with **hard plastic balls**, or **cardboard boxes** that I can climb in and out, or the insides of loo rolls. I like it best when tasty treats are hidden inside them, so I have to work out how to get them.

If you let me, I'll **follow** you around the house or garden. I'll make soft **honking** noises to let you know how happy I am. If I'm allowed out of my cage in the home, make sure that electrical wires and phone cables are out of my reach. I do tend to **nibble** things to see if I can eat them.

I can be clumsy and bump into things. Make sure all your precious ornaments are out of the way before you let me out. I don't want to have an accident!

When I'm hungry

I do like to eat a lot of food and I need lots of vegetables to keep me healthy. I can be a fussy eater as I like very fresh food that smells good. Rabbit pellets are available at pet shops and have a good mix of the vitamins and minerals I need, but I need lots of fresh hay and vegetables to make me grow strong and healthy. Be careful not to give me too many pellets as I might eat them all and then I'll get fat.

Make sure I always have plenty of clean, fresh water to drink.

I like a lot of **different foods**, and can get bored if you don't give me a mixture. I won't eat if I'm bored, and then I'll get ill. I do like **timothy hay** and will eat that every day. It should smell fresh and have a greenish colour, and helps my digestion. Old hay is not good for me. The dust can make me sneeze.

Putting a mineral lick in my cage is a good idea. This means I can get any minerals that might not be in my food.

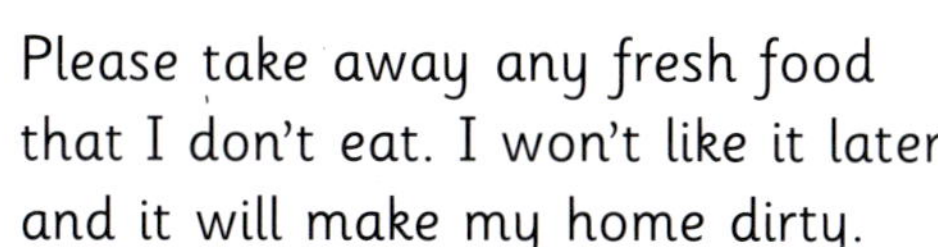

I suffer from tummy upsets if I eat too many **greens**, but I need to have a few each day. Give them to me in the morning, so that I can digest them properly.

I also like some plants that you think of as weeds. I'll eat **dandelion leaves**, **clover**, **cow parsley** and **knapweed**. I also like acorns and black cherries as a treat – but not if they've been sprayed with pesticides.

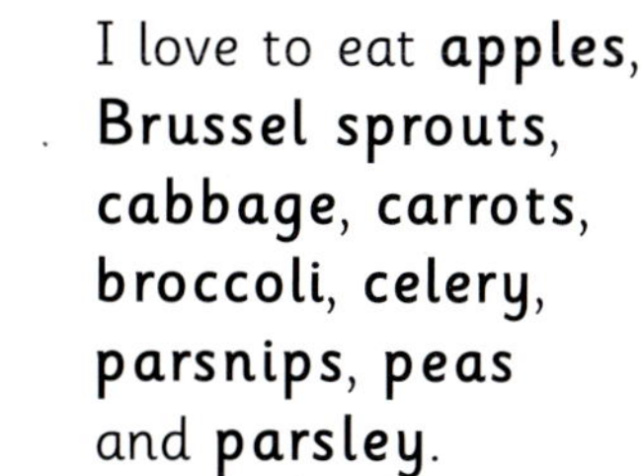

Please take away any fresh food that I don't eat. I won't like it later and it will make my home dirty.

I love to eat **apples**, **Brussel sprouts**, **cabbage**, **carrots**, **broccoli**, **celery**, **parsnips**, **peas** and **parsley**.

When I'm happy

You'll know when we're happy because we look relaxed and content. We'll chatter to you in our own way, and can even whistle if we're excited to see you. If we like you, we will lick your hand in greeting, or give you a gentle push with our head.

If we're sitting on the ground and I snuggle into you, this means that I'm very pleased to see you and love your company.

If we sit up on our **haunches**, it gives us the chance to look around. We can see, hear and smell what's going on so we'll find you if you've wandered off without us.

When we're **very happy**, we make a **purring** sound, like a cat. It means you can keep stroking us. If you're playing with us, we sometimes **grind our teeth**. This is just to show you that we're happy.

We **scratch** at the floor when we want some **attention**. Sometimes we do this if we're thinking about making a burrow. You'll have to find something to catch our attention to stop us.

When our **ears** are **folded back** and we're squatting on the ground, we're very happy and enjoying life. We **jump** on our hind legs and **bounce** up and down when we're excited. We like to see what's going on and we don't like to be left out of the fun.

Keep away!

I can get tired and a bit grumpy at times. If a lot of people have been stroking me and making a fuss of me, I might find it too much and want to be alone. Usually I'll try to be polite and push your hand away, to let you know when I've had enough. If that doesn't work I might nip you with my teeth.

If I get scared, I might lie flat on my tummy with my ears folded back close to my body.

When I get **tense**, I stretch my head and ears forwards to help me concentrate. I'm usually a bit **nervous** when I do this, so if you can talk to me, or gently let me know you're there, I'll relax a bit.

If I grunt at you, it means move away! I'll also **stomp my feet** to let you know when I'm cross.

Male rabbits like to keep others out of their space. If two get together, they may **fight**. These fights can be serious and they can hurt each other.

If a new rabbit is brought into the house, I might get **cross** and try to **fight** it. It's best if you let us get to know each other slowly. Let the newcomer stay in a separate cage close to mine for a few days, so I get used to its smell.

If ever you hear me scream, please come and help. It means I'm in pain or am very frightened. It usually means that something is attacking me and I need help to get away.

When I'm tired

Like all rabbits, I'm most active at dusk and dawn, so I'll be very pleased to see you first thing in the morning and then again in the early evening. I like to rest and sleep a lot at other times.

You'll know when I'm tired because I stop trying to play and just look for a quiet spot to rest in. I sometimes just lie down where I am with my body flat against the ground. My eyes will only be half open, so you'll know I want a nap.

At night, I'll go to the **sleeping** part of my hutch. I need a thick layer of hay in here to keep me **warm** and **cosy**. If it's really cold outside, I can need a whole **bale of hay** to keep me warm. When I'm really tired, I just **stretch** out and **lie** on my side.

If I'm lying down with my back legs sticking out, this means that I'm either tired or hot. Don't try to play with me, as I'd rather be left alone right now.

You can use **sawdust**, **straw**, **shredded paper** or **hay** for my bedding. I prefer hay as I can nibble on it if I get hungry in the night. Don't use really fine sawdust for my bed. The bits can get in my eyes and make them sore.

Washing and grooming

I always like to look my best and try to keep my fur clean and tidy at all times. Usually I can do this by myself, but I do enjoy it when my owner brushes me. If you use a brush with medium bristles it feels lovely. It helps keep my fur in tip-top condition and gives my skin a bit of a massage at the same time. I'll let you know that I like it by chattering to you. But do be gentle!

I can't keep my **hutch clean**, so you'll have to do that. I need my droppings clearing up every day and the whole hutch will need to be scrubbed out once a week. Then I'll need **clean bedding** as well.

Angora rabbits like my friend Hamish, have **very long hair**. They are not very good at keeping clean and tidy and need their humans to help them. It is very important to **brush** an Angora rabbit's coat **every day** to stop it getting **tangled** and **matted**. Luckily, Angoras love being made a fuss of, and really enjoy this grooming.

Some people collect the Angora's hair, which is lovely and soft. It can be spun into a long thread that can be used to make clothes for people to wear. Get a specially trained person to shear or pluck the rabbit, if you want to collect its fur.

If I groom too much or swallow too much of my hair, it can get stuck inside me. I can't be sick, so the hair just stays there. This can make me ill and I have to go the vet.

Every week, I need my **teeth** and **toenails checked**. My teeth grow all the time, and I need hard foods to gnaw on to keep wearing them down. If they get too long, I won't be able to eat properly and I'll get sick. In the wild, I would chew food for about four hours a day and this helps keep my mouth healthy. If my teeth are too long, or I'm having trouble eating, take me to the vet.

My toenails can also grow too long if I don't have hard surfaces to walk over and wear them down. If they get too long, they can hurt my feet when I walk. The vet will be able to show you how to trim them to keep me in good condition.

Keeping healthy

We're usually very healthy and don't get ill very much at all. But sometimes we might have an accident, or get sick and then we do need to see a vet. It's a good idea to take us to the vet once a year for a check up to make sure we're fit and well.

If we start to lose weight, or go off our food, take us to the vet. We might have a fur ball, or parasites might be living inside us. Always take us to the vet if we have diarrhoea.

Be **very careful** when you pick me up or carry me. My back isn't that strong and will break quite easily. If I struggle to get away and you drop me, I can hurt myself really badly.

When you're brushing me, check my skin for any **lumps** or **bumps**. These can be **abscesses** that will need treating. I need to go to the vet if you find these.

Check my **nose** from time to time. It should be **twitchy** and **clean**. If it's snotty or sore looking, I might have an infection. I need to go to the vet urgently.

When I go outside, I can pick up parasites in my fur. These are unwelcome visitors that make me itchy and bad-tempered. Your vet will be able to recommend a special powder to get rid of them.

I can get **ear mites** in my ears. These are **itchy** and make me scratch my ears until they bleed. My ears might get infected and sore, so I need treatment at the vet.

Sometimes I scratch under my chin and then stamp my feet. Don't worry about this, I have a scent gland under my chin and I'm just using the scent to mark my territory.

Pleased to meet you!

I'm a friendly animal and like to live with other animals. I get lonely if I'm left on my own for a long time. The trouble is that I will fight new animals, if I don't know them. So it can be tricky introducing me to new creatures.

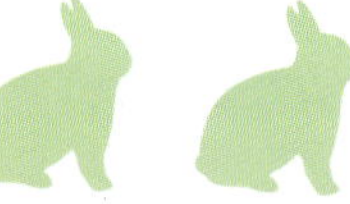

It's best to **introduce** me to other creatures when we're all quite **young**. Dogs usually chase me and try to eat me, so I'm often scared of them. But if I get to know them, we can become friends. Even so, please don't leave me alone with a cat or a dog – it might forget its manners!

If I have a very **large hutch**, I can easily live with another female rabbit or a neutered male. We'll get along if we have enough room and have known each other all our lives. Getting two or more rabbits from the same litter is ideal.

Male rabbits will **fight** each other from about eight weeks old. If they are neutered, they become less grumpy and make better pets.

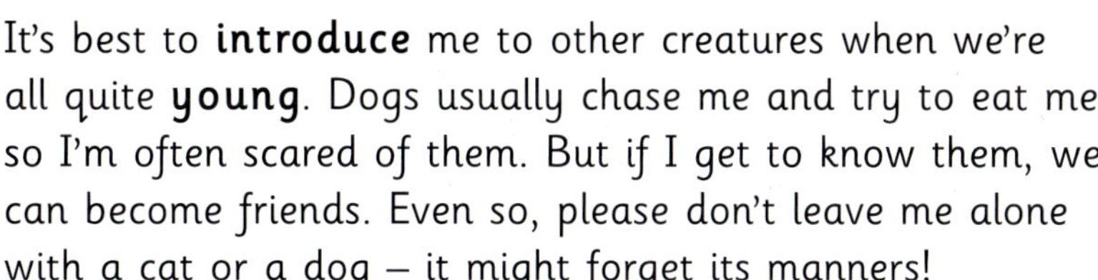

Female rabbits are less likely to fight each other, and will live happily together.

Guinea pigs are good companions too, provided we have a big enough hutch. Be careful though, as if I'm in a bad mood, or if the hutch is too small, I can squash or stamp on the guinea pig.

If your family has **very young children**, or they come to visit, I'll be pleased to come and say hello. But please don't leave me alone with them. They can make me over-excited and then I can get a bit grumpy.

Goodbye!

I've loved writing this book;
I hope it's helped you understand
what makes me happy!

Lulu

FIND OUT MORE

Some useful websites:

www.pdsa.org.uk

www.bbc.co.uk/cbbc/wild/pets

www.allaboutpets.org.uk